STEALTH RACING

About the Author

Rick Smith has over forty years of racing experience at distances ranging from 400 meters to the marathon. He gained his expertise mainly in Massachusetts and Idaho, with brief stints in Kansas and Oregon. He now lives in central New Jersey.

Rick's modest achievements include:

- Class C Massachusetts High School Cross-Country Champion
- Class C Massachusetts High School Indoor Mile Champion
- Fourth Place in the Mile at the Massachusetts State All-Class High School Outdoor Championships
- Third Place in the 1000 yards at the New England Indoor Collegiate Championships
- Four-time Indoor National Sub-Masters Champion and Former Meet Record Holder in the 800 meters

STEALTH RACING

Running Strategy Your Coach Doesn't Know

By Rick Smith

ISBN: 978-1-938545-05-4 (print)
ISBN: 978-1-938545-06-1 (ebook)

For information about permissions, bulk purchases, or additional distribution, write to

Pangea Books
P. O. Box 818
South Orange, NJ 07079
or contact the publisher at
www.pangeabooks.net

For David and Nathan

Table of Contents

Contents

Author's Note

What this book is NOT:

This book is NOT about workouts.

This book is NOT about shoes.

NOT about nutrition.

NOT about race results.

Or apparel.

Your coach probably knows about these things. This is what your coach doesn't know about RACING. Smart training and smart racing are separate skills, and they SHOULD be kept separate. When it's time to race, forget about your training. This book is about what happens when it's time to RACE.

If your races are going well, this book is not for you. If it ain't broke, don't fix it, right? Come back when it's broke.

Introduction

Half the people who learn about stealth racing WON'T want to do it.

Half of those who WANT to do it CAN'T do it.

Half of those who CAN do it will STOP doing it.

That's okay. Stealth racing works best if you are the only one doing it.

Stealth racing is for those who want to know WHAT happens in a race, WHY it happens, and WHAT to do about it.

> **Stealth racing is for those who want to know WHAT happens in a race, WHY it happens, and WHAT to do about it.**

If you think a race is ONLY a test of character and a measure of self-worth, you will hate stealth racing.

Running is a sport. And like other sports, it's all about enjoying the thrill of competing, not dreading the thought of it.

When the races go well the training gets easier. The pressure is off. Stealth racing makes the races go easier. Is that a bad thing? I don't think so.

So even if you aren't a stealth racer, you may be able to learn from one. You can pick and choose what you want to use in your races. It's up to you what you do with the content of this book. I highly suggest that you keep it stealth.

This leads to the first rule of stealth racing: DON'T CALL IT STEALTH RACING!

> **The first rule of stealth racing: DON'T CALL IT STEALTH RACING**

We don't need idiots screwing up stealth racing because it sounds cool. What part of the word "stealth" isn't understood? If you don't know what the word "stealth" means, google it.

If asked if you are a stealth racer, just give them some lame answer that will make them go away. "No, I just got lucky." "I've got to learn to race better than that." Most people are clueless; it doesn't take much to keep them that way.

Also, you don't need the scrutiny or the pressure. It only takes a couple of races to figure out if stealth racing works for you.

Rick Smith

July, 2015

STEALTH RACING

1
Why Stealth

WHAT IT IS

Now, ONLY a stealth racer knows that to WATCH a race is to WATCH an optical illusion. The strategy remains hidden in plain sight.

> *The strategy remains hidden in plain sight.*

The best runners can run a race any way they want as long as they win. Non-winners have no such luxury. They should. Every racer becomes a non-winner at some point. Stealth racing prepares you for when this happens.

A few sales pitches before we begin.

Stealth racing may be for you if:

- What USED to work for you no longer works.
- What worked ONCE for you won't work again.

- What ALWAYS worked for you didn't work that one time you needed it.

Stealth racing is a structured approach to racing, NOT a collection of assorted tactics. A good tactic used in the wrong situation will only hurt the performance of the one using it. The right strategy often (not always) makes the use of tactics unnecessary.

Stealth racing is that strategy.

In stealth racing, the most important focus in a race is to get to the finish line in the least amount of time. What happens on the way to getting there is secondary. When did you ever hear racing described THAT way?

> *The most important focus is to get to the finish line in the least amount of time. What happens on the way to getting there is secondary.*

Stealth racing teaches you what is important in a race AND what is less important in a race. The keys are mostly the same, it's the priorities that get mixed up.

The strategy is simple. Everyone knows it. Almost no one does it. They just think that they do it. In fact, if you are the only one doing it in a race, YOU will be the only one accused of NOT doing it!

The principle is simple. The screw-ups are endless. When you know the key, everything else falls into place.

What is that key?

PACE YOURSELF - EVENLY!

So. You're still reading? I think half of the readers just stopped.

Not only is stealth racing hidden behind an optical illusion, it's hidden under one big yawn of a description. It's one more thing you can tell people who ask you what you're doing. Tell them the truth. "I'm just trying to pace myself." "Oh. Okay."

> ***PACE YOURSELF - EVENLY!***

NO SCIENCE, JUST MATH

No science here in stealth racing. You have to take someone's word that they are right about the science. Stealth racing is math. Everyone who does the math correctly comes up with the same answer.

Do the math (or find someone who can.) Take your two best racing distances where one race is twice as long as the other. (Aren't almost all of them?) What's the difference in pace between the two races? It's about 10%. (More for long sprints, less for long distance races.)

Do you realize what that means? If you speed up 10%, you go through your energy TWICE as fast. It takes a LOT of energy to go a LITTLE faster.

What if your car ran that way? You drive 55 mph instead of 50 mph and you only go half as far. How do you even race a vehicle that is so speed-sensitive? You had better watch your speed (your pace.)

IT DOESN'T COME NATURALLY

Athletes bring in habits from other sports to running. Some work. A lot don't. The biggest one that won't work is aggressiveness. Concentration and relaxation are the way to go.

It is natural to run aggressively. It is the natural use for running. RUNNING A RACE IS NOT NATURAL!

RUNNING A RACE IS NOT NATURAL!

Natural runners don't RACE, they CHASE. Or they FLEE. Racing all over an athletic field, or up and down a court, is where you race naturally. But NOT in a race.

What's the difference? A STARTING line and a FINISH line. ESPECIALLY if they are more than 35 to 40 seconds apart. (The fields in sports aren't that big.)

The NATURAL use for running (chasing or fleeing) ends if someone gets caught, either on the athletic field, or with a cheetah and a gazelle on the plains of Africa.

The cheetah doesn't line up with the gazelle and say, "First one to the end of the next field gets to eat the other." NO! RUNNING A RACE IS NOT NATURAL! A race ends at the finish line, NOT when someone gets caught.

This fear of not catching someone leads to the WORST tactic to the stealth racer: Maintain contact with the leader.

The WORST tactic to the stealth racer: Maintain contact with the leader.

NO! Maintain contact with an even pace!

Since I'm mentioning instincts brought in from other sports, there is no quarterback waiting in the infield ready to throw a game ending touchdown pass to your "uncovered" opponent. Your competitor is not charging uncontested toward your goalie for an open shot. Let him go. This is not a game. This is a race. The ONLY time position matters is when you are at the finish line, not before.

What does the fastest runner (at that moment) and everyone who is chasing him have to do with YOU getting to the finish line in the least amount of time? Your best chance for success is to NOT make the same mistake that other runners often make which is chasing someone who is faster than you. A lot of races are even won by the runner who resists chasing the lead pack when the early pace is too fast.

And the BEST chance of beating a BETTER runner is if you don't make mistakes that other runner is more likely to make. Usually, that mistake is running too FAST, NOT running too SLOW.

Some runners have discovered that running from behind can be quite successful as a tactic. Until it isn't. That's when potential stealth racers STOP being stealth racers.

The "stealth" in stealth racing happens at this point. What point? When a race goes out slow.

Second rule of stealth racing: IGNORE YOUR COMPETITORS! ESPECIALLY at the start!

Second rule: IGNORE YOUR COMPETITORS!

THE EVEN PACE PARADOX

You begin by first ignoring other runners when they start too fast. They almost always start too fast. The surprise happens when they start too slow.

If everyone is too afraid to lead the race, the stealth racer doesn't care. The stealth racer has a pace to run. The stealth racer will take the lead. This usually results in everyone chasing the stealth racer, waiting for him to die (that means slow down for those of you who are new to running lingo.)

But it's usually ONLY the stealth racer who knows that to maintain an even pace requires a GRADUALLY INCREASING effort. The stealth racer accounts for this. The others usually don't. The stealth racer DOESN'T die. Everyone chasing the stealth racer usually DOES.

It's after the race when the stealth racer finds out his strategy is safe. Spectators say: "Wow, you looked strong out there!" "You looked confident." "You took

21

command of the race and just pulled away." "That's not like you usually race." "You usually sit in back and try to run people down."

The stealth racer knows he did the same thing he always does: run an even pace to an ALL OUT performance.

It was the other runners (the pack) who did something different. It was the behavior of the MANY (the pack) that changed the look of the strategy of the ONE (you.)

The stealth racer now knows that his strategy is safely concealed behind the optical illusion. It remains hidden in plain sight when people describe his "tactic" in completely opposite terms when he employs the same stealth strategy.

Okay now. "All this fuss about how to race and all you've got is even pace?" Yes. "Don't most people race that way?" No. If they do, it is usually by accident.

Some runners think that they've paced themselves if they can get to the finish line without walking! There is wide discrepancy for what people think when they hear the term "even." Remember, 10% faster equals TWICE the fatigue. Even 5% can get a little ugly

(3 seconds per minute.) Why make yourself more tired when it's not even helping your performance?

STEALTH VS. NATURAL

I'll tell you why most runners do it. It's from the perspective of the consistently run stealth race that you can begin to spot all the mistakes of the natural runner.

First, you can't SEE even pace. (Many refer to this as race pace. Somehow, almost all runners only run race pace in workouts, NOT in races.) If you do even pace in a race, it looks WRONG. It's scary. It looks too SLOW. Especially at the start.

Second, it FEELS wrong. It's too easy. "This is a RACE, I should be working HARDER than THIS!"

Everyone pushes themselves when they are tired. Can you refrain from going faster when the best pace feels too slow?

Can you refrain from going faster when the best pace feels too slow?

Once again, it takes an increasing effort to maintain an even pace. Even pace during a race is a COMPLETELY DIFFERENT rhythm. A CONSTANT fatigue level equals a gradually SLOWING pace. THAT is the rhythm of the NATURAL runner.

A stealth racer starts with striding. A stealth racer finishes with the "pedal to the floor." A stealth racer times it so that he hits the finish line as he has reduced himself to running on "fumes."

How slowly can you push your "gas pedal" to the floor?

The natural runner doesn't have this skill. The natural runner hits fatigue sooner. To make it to the finish, he has to back off of his pace too early.

The stealth racer times it so that he hits the fatigue level later. He can push through the fatigue level HARDER because he pushes for a shorter time. His greatest fatigue occurs when he is passing natural runners quickly. Great fatigue is no problem when these natural runners are like dying rabbits in front of him.

Stealth racing is both easier and harder. Easier when it is supposed to be. Harder when you want it to be. It's just different. And better. And NOT natural.

A quick "philosophical" break before getting to more details on HOW to race.

I know you runners eat this stuff up, I've been to your meets, I've seen the slogans on your t-shirts.

Ever hear the phrase, "keeping up with the Joneses?" It's a common trap in life to try to keep up appearances so that you don't look inferior compared to someone else. You usually can't know what it is costing somebody to LOOK better than you. How much are they going into debt to have those things that you don't have?

Similarly, in a race, you can't always tell how much that runner up front is going into oxygen debt to look good. Running your own race (who hasn't heard THAT phrase before?) now makes a lot more sense in this context.

Let them go. If they ARE that good, it doesn't make sense to destroy your race pretending to have abilities that you don't. If they are NOT that good, you can take your shot when they go "bankrupt." The great thing is, you can SEE this happen right in front of you. (The natural runner just doesn't see the things that the stealth racer gets to see.)

After a while, the stealth racer doesn't even have to see it, he just knows it. The actions of the natural runner become all too predictable. Predicting the mistakes of the natural runner endlessly entertains the stealth racer during his races. As you become the stealth racer, YOU begin to know the factors that cause the mistakes of the natural runner. YOU are the runner who knows what you are doing.

If your race doesn't go well, YOU are the one looking forward to the next race because YOU know how to fix it. YOU know that what other runners do with their bodies has little impact on what YOU do with your body. YOU don't fall into the trap that they do.

Worrying about WHAT you see.

Caring about HOW it looks.

Natural runners are ruled by what they SEE. They would rather FEEL bad (tired) than LOOK bad (trailing in back.)

> *Natural runners are ruled by what they SEE.*

Stealth racers focus on what they feel. It is information. It is the one sense that isn't controlled by the other runners.

Excuse me, if a legally blind runner can make it to the Olympics in the 1500 meters, SIGHT is a very,

very, very overrated sense when it comes to running a race. Ignore, ignore, ignore what you see.

Unless, of course, it's just too much fun to ignore.

If FUN is what you like, nothing beats stealth racing. It is the bungee jump of race strategies.

> *If FUN is what you like, nothing beats stealth racing.*

Try to let go of everything familiar, let go of everything the natural runners do. Just run an even pace to an all out performance and get ready for the multiple reactions you will get from the crowd, the coach, your teammates, your family, and even your competitors. The reactions may not all be positive, but they can get LOUD.

2
First Stealth Race

KEEP IT SIMPLE

A quick recap of the reasons why almost no runners race at an even pace:

- They can't see even pace.
- Even pace feels wrong at the start.
- Even pace sounds boring.

> *A quick recap WHY so few race at an even pace: They can't see it, it feels wrong, it sounds boring.*

All you need to do now is find out for yourself how "unboring" your races will become.

Now the best description of the mindset of the stealth racer is: IT IS LIKE RUNNING A TIME TRIAL WHILE A RACE IS GOING ON. This is the simplest (and the best) wording of the strategy to attempt your first stealth race.

There is a lot of information in this book, but you can't race well with an overloaded brain. The "time trial" mindset is best for eliminating most distractions in your race. Accuracy in pace becomes the main focus in producing your best result for your race on that particular day. Chasing some dream time is the wasteland of the natural runner.

The stealth racer is more focused on predicting his time accurately and dealing with reality. If he underestimates his ability, he is in for a happy "accident." (What? Having too big of a kick is some terrible disaster? He can recalculate for his next race.)

Once again, stealth racing is math. When running your first stealth race, it is important to get early feedback on pace. Get it at 100 meters where you can correct pacing mistakes quickly.

So take your predicted time (in seconds) and divide it by the number of hundreds of meters that is the length of your race. (Example: 5000 meters, divide by 50.) If you can, it MAY be helpful to practice the feel of this tempo by timing it on a track. In your particular case it may be an alert to how slow or easy it is, maybe not. The REALITY is that running in a race usually feels different than striding in a workout, even if the pace is exactly the same.

Adrenaline (or "butterflies" — that queasy nervous feeling in your gut) can have an effect. Refer ahead to the five psychological factors of a particular race to anticipate how much this could affect you.

There is a limit to the usefulness of practicing the pace. You need to race to learn how to race.

THE EASY START

You are not going to be exact on your pace anyway, so know that it is better to be too slow on your start than to be too fast. There are a number of reasons for this.

Being too fast is difficult to correct. Being too slow is easy to correct.

Also, starting too slow hurts your performance only HALF as much as starting too fast. If the natural runner hears his split time is three seconds fast, he thinks, "Great, I'm three seconds ahead of pace!" What he doesn't realize is that he's probably six seconds behind on energy.

Too fast is difficult to correct. Too slow is easy to correct.

For your first attempt at an even paced race, it is best to have someone get your split time at 100 meters and call it out to you immediately (whole seconds are usually not exact enough, get it to the nearest tenth, if you can.) Also make sure you get regular interval splits recorded for the rest of the race (four to eight should be enough at conveniently marked spots.)

If your time is too slow, it is easy to increase your effort. Your first split technically should be slower because you lose a few tenths during your acceleration from the fully stopped position on the starting line. The other splits have a running start. If your split is too fast, it can be difficult to back off a bit and then resume at the correct pace. It kind of messes up your attempt to find the right rhythm.

Most important of all, an even pace is NOT something that you SETTLE INTO. It is a very gradual ACCELERATION of effort as you face gradually INCREASING fatigue to maintain your even pace.

> ***An even pace is NOT something that you SETTLE INTO.***

Don't do the 100 meter split routine more than once unless you really screw it up the first time. It can be difficult to race and think at the same time (though longer races do allow more time for thinking.) In shorter races, if your thoughts can't take the form of pictures in your mind, physical sensations, or can't be expressed in short simple phrases, it can be tough to get the level of relaxation you need.

Always do your analyzing AFTER your race. Otherwise, you could end up "riding the brake" and "pushing the accelerator" at the same time. If you focus too much on your splits during the race, you can become tense and waste energy that way. Getting your splits at least within 2% of each other should be good enough, with negative splits more preferable at first. Your first attempt might feel awkward but usually your time doesn't suffer.

It is in the days between your first and second stealth race when your subconscious starts to get it. By the time you get to your next race, you will stand at the starting line surprisingly knowing what you are doing. Your brain has assimilated all of the information and experience from the first attempt and simplified it into a rhythm.

You will enjoy this race because you will be relaxed, it will feel good, and it will be faster. You will have made the transition from running a race expecting to be rewarded for your effort, to racing where you will be rewarded for the result. For a lot of runners, running for the appreciation of their effort is their whole motivation for running. The stealth racer leaves them alone. They are the runners who make him look good, and his strategy look exciting.

NAVIGATING COMMON DIFFICULTIES

There is another important reason for the 100 meter split time, and preferring too slow rather than too fast. It messes up the math.

When you think about it, what you are trying to accomplish appears quite difficult. You want an even pace, and at the finish you want an "empty tank."

You don't have a speedometer. You don't have a fuel gauge.

So you have to "feel" your fuel gauge. At first you don't know what an evenly paced race feels like, so as you get better at it, you should immediately focus on memorizing the feel. (You may not ALWAYS get accurate splits during your races.) Also, you can't really SEE your speed (your vision gets tricked into focusing on the relative speed of the other runners.)

So instead of speed, you get information from your split times. But, (this is an important detail,) a split time does NOT indicate your CURRENT speed. Splits indicate your AVERAGE speed over the length of the whole interval.

Let me explain why this is an important distinction during the beginning of a race.

You may have already experienced this type of scenario: Let's say you would like to run 800 meters in 2:20 on an indoor 200 meter track. That means you want to hear "35" after one lap (2:20 pace.) So you "pop" off the starting line, sprint to the front of the pack, and settle in (let's say this is a relatively fast high school girl.)

But you lead the other runners through the first lap in 34 seconds. You think, "Great, I can do it this time!" You are completely settled into your rhythm, you are coming up to the halfway point at 400 meters, you are expecting to hear "68" (1:08, half of 2:16!) Instead, you hear "71!" (half of 2:22!)

Frustrated, or confused, you push the third 200, try to kick in the last 200, and end up with a 2:24. You never want to be bothered with splits again. What happened?

> ***You never want to bother with split times again. What happened?***

You remember that harmless little "pop" off the starting line? It was a short, quick sprint to the front that put you through the first 100 meters in, let's say, 16 seconds. Your "settled in" pace brought you through 200 meters at 34 seconds, so you ran that second 100 in 18 seconds. At 200 meters, you think your current pace is 34 seconds per lap. It is actually 36 (2 X 18.) And since you have "settled in" at that effort level (a gradually slowing pace,) your second lap isn't even a 36, but a 37 (which gives you your 71.) You increased your effort on the third 200, which maintained your 37-second-pace, then kicked in with a 36. 34 + 37 + 37 + 36 = 144 = 2:24. Scenario explained.

So how does the 2:24 runner make the adjustment to a stealth race?

Run the first 100 in 18 seconds, not 16. That 2 seconds puts you well back in the pack. Relax. Keep running 18s as you pick off one or two runners. Usually around the back stretch of the third lap is where the pack begins to slow. That's where you might throw in a surge to move up. You CAN surge because you have the energy in reserve from slowing that start down 2 seconds. It's now clear sailing to the finish as you usually pick off the last runners at your leisure, and maybe bury everyone with a kick.

Going forward from an approximate 2:23 or 2:22, the stealth racer, with extra anticipation, relaxation, and confidence, can click a few more seconds off. Maybe just run 17.5s all the way. Maybe that 2:20 will happen after all.

If your race is a leg of a relay, make sure your split-taker times the BATON as it crosses the line that marks the correct distance and NOT at the exchange of the baton. A baton pass can happen early or late in the exchange zone and alter the measure of the split by entire seconds and render them useless for measuring pace and performance.

PACING OFF THE TRACK

If your first race is a cross-country race, your task may be a bit harder. Not all miles are equal on a cross-country course and this SHOULD show in your split times. The biggest factor is hills, but sometimes the footing or number of turns can have an effect that will slow your pace. Check the "Hills" section of the book for more on that.

Usually (but not always) at least the start of the course is flat and that is the MOST important part of a stealth race. There are different approaches you can take depending on your math skills (or those of a teammate or friend.)

Having someone yell out the precise time in seconds at the 1/60th point of the race will correspond to your finish time pace in minutes. This might only work for a 5K (5000 meter) course and this point is always at 83 1/3 meters (or 91 yards). On courses where this is not the case (the exact length is not known or not precisely measured) you may be familiar enough with your 5k time that this information is sufficient.

Also, you could find out which of your teammates start at your race pace and follow them off of the starting line. Most cross-country runners start off the line at least one minute per mile under their race pace. The fast start is an important habit to break as a stealth racer. It is your first step in ignoring your competitors.

> *The fast start is an important habit to break as a stealth racer.*

The MOST important thing is to understand the concept. Start slow and gradually increase your effort to maintain your speed. If done correctly, you'll find that a slow speed won't feel slow for long.

Even though this book is NOT about workouts, there are skills you can practice DURING your workouts.

(During any workout with hills, you can practice the rhythm of hill running described in the later chapter.)

There also is a way you can practice the rhythm or feel of stealth racing in a useful way without worrying about the math. If alone, you can choose any short loop with any terrain and time yourself as you run consecutive laps around the same course. You first focus only on getting your time per loop as close to the SAME time as you can (don't worry about how FAST it is — this is more of a racing skills practice than a workout.) Leave a small zone at the end of the loop where you can take a second or two (while still jogging) to stop your stopwatch, look at your time, reset, and start it again as you cross your start line for the next timed loop.

The purpose of this exercise is to train your body to get in the habit of running at the same pace, NOT the same effort level. You will find that a comfortable pace becomes a workout pace after only a few of these laps. As an extra benefit, you will find that more and more your natural reaction to fatigue will be to ACCELERATE your effort instead of backing off on your pace. Having this instinct is very useful as you get closer to the finish line in races. You are more likely to produce the more effective long sustaining drive to the finish instead of the quick sprint kick that leaves you with too much unspent energy.

I will now give you EIGHT factors to consider when you enter any race. They should give you some clue as to what you are getting yourself into when you run a stealth race. There are racing scenarios where a lot of runners will actually race at an even pace. Change enough of the conditions for these runners and an even pace becomes a rarity. The natural runner is usually unaware of any of these factors.

There are three PHYSICAL factors, and five PSYCHOLOGICAL factors. Since this book also functions as a handbook, there will be some repetition of concepts as they apply to more than one of these factors, but are set in a different context.

Other points are repeated on purpose to stress how stealth racing is different. These are key phrases that you want foremost in your mind if defending your actions becomes necessary. Friends, family, teammates, and coaches should sometimes be clued in to what you are doing so that they can enjoy being a spectator to your performances.

The following chapters should reveal most mistakes of the natural runner. And after all, isn't that how we all get started? As natural runners?

3
Physical Race Factors

LENGTH OF RACE

There are five "zones" to consider for the length of your race.

Races That Last 4 to 40 Seconds

Sprint away! The true definition of a sprint is determined by the time, not the length, of the race. (Picture a 5-year-old trying to sprint an entire 200-meter race. It won't be a sprint.) Sprinting is not determined by speed. (If you can stride faster than someone else can sprint, you're still not sprinting, no matter how glowing their description.)

When you are sprinting all out, you will not run out of "gas" for 35 seconds if you are relaxed. If you do, it is because you are too tight. Maybe you should NOT be sprinting.

Stealth racing is of no value in true sprint races.

Up to 40 seconds, it doesn't matter if you do run out of "gas," your momentum will carry you across the finish line if you maintain form.

Stealth racing is of no value in true sprint races. However, it can be of great value if your races go just a little bit longer.

Races That Last 40 to 60 Seconds

For the stealth racer, this is the transition zone between sprinting a race and pacing a race. For the sprinter who is reluctant to run races that are these longer sprints, or long sprinters who attempt middle distances, stealth racing offers a more pleasant way to adjust to these potentially "painful" races.

> *Stealth racing offers a more pleasant way to adjust to these potentially "painful" races.*

Don't worry about your time on your first attempt. Just start with "floating" through the first half of the race, and then "flying" through the last half of the race. That shouldn't hurt, should it? Have someone get your splits because you will be surprised how even they will be. Initially, it is more important to LIKE the new, longer distance.

Too many sprinters throw in the towel after one attempt. Give yourself a break. It usually takes three or four races to "install" this new gear. Give yourself the time while your body finds its "groove."

Racing at any new distance is not as easy as it seems. It can be difficult to get at all your body is capable of. The first time is the worst. Successive attempts get easier.

In the 45 to 50 second range you can still be considered "stealth" if you can keep the time for your last half within a second of the time for your first half. These are mostly 400 meter races at this point. Very, very few 400 meter runners do this. Some 400 meter hurdlers are more likely to do this out of necessity.

At some point, it just seems like a good idea to even-split an open 400 meter race so you can see how much time you lose by pacing evenly. It is probably much less than expected, and the experience could greatly reduce the panic factor during races (especially in relays.) Being able to ease off and NOT panic when situations arise (especially indoors) can greatly enhance your tactical skill.

A lot of long sprinters are terrified of getting behind in an indoor race because they think it is too hard to pass. The stealth racer knows that starting a race a little slower is a problem. Starting a LOT slower (even pace) is no problem at all. Let me explain why.

There are three factors to consider when making a successful pass:

First, there is the difference in speed between you and the runner you are attempting to pass. The greater the difference, the quicker (and easier) the pass.

Second, it depends where on the track this is happening: On a long straightaway — no problem. On a short straightaway — a bit of a problem. On a gradual sweeping turn —- a problem. On a short sharp turn — a big problem.

Third, there is the ability of the other runner to speed up and hold you off. Early in the race, it is quite possible for him to do this. Late in the race, it isn't. Late in the race also means it will probably happen on a straightaway.

Oh, by the way, if you want the loudest reaction from a crowd, nothing beats even-splitting an open 400 meter race on an indoor track against runners who are no better than you. Passing runners who, near the end of the race, are going much slower and have no energy, is no problem even on a short sharp turn. You will go from distant last to first so fast, that spectators will HAVE to react because they've probably never seen it before.

Oh, and you might need an "excuse" prepared. The coach might want an explanation. Talk loud, it takes quite a while for a crowd to quiet down.

Outdoor 400 meters? Do whatever you want. They almost always run it in lanes. Nobody can affect your performance if you ignore them. So ignore them. Pace how you want to pace. Find the rhythm that produces your best time.

Races Between 60 Seconds in Time and 800 Meters in Length

This is the center of the stealth racing distances.

Usually the greatest (and scariest) results happen in these races. These are your not-so-fast 400-meter runners, your 500-meter, 600-yard, 600-meter, and 800-meter competitions.

These are the races (a little less so for the 800) that when paced evenly, make you look like a junior varsity athlete at the start, and some sort of Olympian at the end (even though you are not going any faster at the finish than you are at the start.)

Most athletes are stuck in almost a sprint mode at these distances even though they have no way of maintaining their pace. They don't know any other way to compete. They are the ultimate sitting ducks for the stealth racer.

> **They are the ultimate "sitting ducks" for the stealth racer.**

Even in some of the 800-meter races where some of the "greatest kicks of all time" were witnessed, the "kicker" often still runs his last half as much as two seconds SLOWER than his first half! Almost no one notices that all the other runners slowed four, five, or even more seconds. Since they all slowed down together, this again produces the ILLUSION of the one racer speeding up.

The announcer (whose job is to "call it as he sees it") will make some comment about how fortunate this runner was to win with this "risky" strategy. He might even remark that this winning runner who was so far in back was in some kind of "danger zone." The stealth racer knows that the "danger zone" in these very fast paced races is up in front where "rabbits" are running on fumes and dying quickly. It is not in back where a runner will have unspent energy in reserve due to a pace that makes a lot more sense.

Don't get frustrated by how announcers react to possible stealth racers in top competitions, they help keep your strategy secret. (After all, how boring would it be if everyone did stealth racing?)

Here's a big revelation: A kick in races between 400 meters and 800 meters (and sometimes longer) is NOT a function of SPEED, it is a function of ENERGY. A runner with energy and without speed can easily take down a speedy runner without energy.

> *A kick in these races is not a function of speed.*

Don't be discouraged from dropping down to these mid-range races because you think you don't have what it takes. What you don't have may help you.

So save your energy and run even splits. Just don't panic when they leave you in the dust at the start. You WON'T have to catch them, THEY will come back to YOU at an alarming rate. Just don't hit them. Be alert, go around them. There are even more of them ahead between you and the quickly approaching finish line.

Races Between 800 Meters and 10,000 Meters (10K) in Length

Ever wonder why they have rabbits for the mile (and longer) but NEVER for the 800 meters? I'll tell you why. It's the PAIN factor.

It's not the collision-impact-sharp-searing kind of pain. It's the self-inflicted, pillow-over-your-face, I'm-dying-but-I'll-never-give-up, keep-going-going-going, kind of pain. Isn't every race that is not a sprint an exercise in pain tolerance?

The longer the race, the more glaringly apparent this facet of racing becomes. Natural runners do what they feel they must to prepare for this. Stealth racers minimize the effect of pain because they have more important things to think about.

At these distances, you get widely varying racing at the elite level (your televised competitions.) You get fast starts, slow starts, mid-race surges, sprint kicks, etc. Outside of this, you just get natural runners behaving naturally.

On a side note, have you noticed announcers when covering a middle-distance race at an elite televised meet will note that a slow-paced race could become a kicker's race? What they imply is that it could "fall into the hands" of a runner of lesser ability who can sprint faster.

Ever notice how this almost never happens? The best runners usually still win these slow-paced races, whatever their ability for speed. The slower runner with the great speed almost never does. Again, a kick is more a function of energy (which the best runners logically have) and not a function of speed.

And do you also ever notice in some of these slow starting races that often the finishing time is not really that slow? Again, starting a race too slow hurts your time, but only half as much as starting too fast.

Now is a good time to explain with math why this is the case when races start slow.

Take a miler, whose half-mile race pace is 10% faster and his two-mile race pace is 10% slower. Let's say his times for these three distances are 2:06, 4:40, and 10:16. His quarter mile race pace for these distances are 63, 70, and 77 seconds (10% apart, also noted as 1:03, 1:10, and 1:17.)

When racing in the mile, if his first quarter mile is run in 63 seconds, he is essentially burning up half his energy doing so (he is running half of a half-mile at

2:06.) If he then runs his second quarter mile in 70 seconds, he is burning through an additional quarter of his energy (one quarter of his 4:40 mile.) This leaves him with one quarter of his energy to run the last half-mile, which, logically he will run at his two-mile pace (two quarters at 77 seconds equals 2:34) His 7 second too fast start has cost him 7 seconds on his time (1:03 + 1:10 + 2:34 = 4:47.)

If he were to run these splits in reverse order, you would see that he could run his 7 second per quarter too slow start for TWICE as long to hurt his performance as much as his 7 second too fast start. Too fast hurts twice as much as too slow.

Don't go faster than pace early in your race unless you have a good reason. (It's an extra crowded start or you're feeling unusually good.) Sometimes "official" splits aren't accurate because the watch is wrong or the split marker is incorrectly located. What is more important is knowing generally how you should feel at any point in a race.

> *Don't go faster than your race pace, unless you have a reason for doing so.*

It is at the upper end (10K) of this zone where the factor of length in a race disappears. It is more in the PSYCHOLOGICAL realm that the natural runner makes mistakes that the stealth runner is much less likely to make (see the later chapter for more.)

Races Over 10,000 Meters in Length

It is at these distances where even natural runners begin to understand pace. "It's not a sprint, it's a marathon." What? Like there's nothing in between? (I said, "They BEGIN to understand.")

Anyway. So everyone at these distances does have a clue. So what does even pace to an all-out performance (basically THE definition of stealth racing) mean at these distances? This is where the rhythm of the stealth race becomes more important. The FEEL of the even-paced race is roughly divided into the four quarters of a race of any distance.

First quarter —- easy striding. Second quarter —- exert some effort. Third quarter —- time to go to work. Fourth quarter —- gradually increasing pain.

Or if you would like something a little catchier: Kick back. Kick it around. Kick it up. Kick it in.

The longer the race, the longer that last quarter of the race is. The PAIN zone in longer races is LONGER! It really makes sense in longer races to run the first half slower, and the second half faster. (This is what's known as a negative split.)

> *It really makes sense in these longer races to run a negative split.*

Shortening your pain zone can be worth the small amount of time you might sacrifice from your performance. Give yourself a lot more leeway on pace for these longer races that have longer zones of increasing fatigue.

Also, more time can mean that your body can go through different rhythms and cycles during the race. You can experience an occasional bad patch that has nothing to do with pacing. Also, an easy pace can turn harder if you happen to have a bad day.

Since runners have actually died running distance races, caution is always recommended the longer the race and the hotter the temperature. You know how obsessive you competitive runners can sometimes get during a long-distance race. It will make for an easier and more enjoyable racing career (however long it lasts) if you resist the urge to risk your health when you get into some duel in that one race that you think is so important.

Burn out is real in any competitor's career. Knowing how to go all out at an even pace for the ultimate race is a great asset. Knowing when good enough is good enough makes for the longer career. Medical situations eventually take their toll on your body. It isn't worth it. Be careful if this could be you.

4
More Physical Race Factors

LOCATION OF RACE

Indoor vs. Outdoor

There are quite a number of factors to consider when you race indoors as opposed to racing on a 400-meter track outdoors.

Unlike an outdoor track, an indoor track can have varying lengths, degrees of banking, and shapes. The lengths of the track are usually 200 meters or 160 yards, or sometimes something different (like 1/10 of a mile.) The banking in the turns can vary in slope from steep, to moderate, to nothing at all (a flat facility floor.)

The shape of the track can vary. It can be an oval with long straightaways and shorter sharper turns. It can be an oval with short straightaways and gradual sweeping curves. It can be a rectangle with rounded corners. It can even be a combination of these.

The natural runner can get overly excited due to the smaller confines of an indoor arena. The noise and intensity doesn't dissipate as much as at an outdoor facility. The natural runner is also likely to get more panicky about his start because it is more difficult to pass on an indoor track. The natural runner is prone to start much too fast because of the fear of getting "stuck" in the back.

> *It is more difficult to pass on an indoor track.*

The stealth racer has no such fear. He enjoys the comfort of striding his race pace efficiently and unhindered (and usually in back, going the shortest distance on the inside lane.) His fellow competitors are his rabbits, ready to be picked off at his convenience. In shorter races he avoids wasting large amounts of energy fighting the first turn (especially on the sharper, less-banked tracks.) He also avoids all the pre-race jitters just worrying about it.

Racing indoors, the stealth racer also likes that he will probably get twice as many split times recorded for him that he can check after the race. Examining them, he may note some departures from even pace that are expected due to the action occurring during the race, and that no adjustments are needed.

But some departures may alert him to patterns in his perception of what he thought was even pace. He could discover tendencies that he would need to be aware of (see the Psychological Factors chapter later for some possibilities.) On an outdoor track his racing habits could be affected by the weather (temperature alone may alter pace preferences.)

Physical Factors: Hills

This is where I confess that what I mean by "even pace" is even energy output.

> **Even pace is really even energy output.**

In cross country and road races you often have to negotiate hills. On flat tracks, of course, your even energy output equals even pace. The natural runner usually is very uncomfortable with the idea of slowing down on the uphill. All it takes is his coach saying, "Attack the hills," and the natural runner won't think twice.

The stealth runner resists the urge. Why throw in a surge of effort in the middle of your race? Unless you have a very specific reason for blowing out a lot of your very precious energy, don't do it. After all, in a race, WHAT ELSE DO YOU HAVE BUT YOUR ENERGY?

> *In a race, WHAT ELSE DO YOU HAVE BUT YOUR ENERGY?*

The stealth racer makes up for the slower climb up the hills by easily returning to speed on the flats. Not only that, but on longer hills he makes up for the slower ascent on the bottom half of the hill by maintaining his pace and catching the natural runner on the top half of the hill. He then destroys the natural runner on the flats.

In an effort to prove how tough he is, the natural runner ruins his race.

NEWS FLASH to all coaches and runners: Every one of us is tough! Let me quote another t-shirt: "Our sport is your sport's punishment." Where do we get the idea that any runner is lazy? Lazy people don't run!

Most runners have to resist their natural urge to over-train, over-race, and over-everything in their lives. Running a race is NOT natural. What runners need are the unnatural habits of consistency and patience. Running a race is a sport. It is not an arena for martyrdom.

> *Running a race is a sport. It is not an arena for martyrdom.*

Don't worry about looking lazy in comparison. Natural runners will sacrifice their bodies chasing their dreams. Stealth racers just run down dying dream-chasers. Which one are you?

Downhill is a different problem. Any downhill is a forced recovery in the middle of your attempt to keep your energy expenditure consistent. It doesn't take much slope to put you into this situation. Learn to let go on the downhill. Just don't trash your legs in the process. Practice it every time you run downhill. But don't overdo it, a little goes a long way.

Unlike running uphill, there is an art to running downhill. Speed is an asset when you really let go on a downhill. If you have limited speed, you can experiment with longer and longer strides. You may have the leg strength to handle faster descents that way.

You can also put in a little surge before the downhill to make the recovery you are forced to experience more tolerable.

The natural runner generally slows down about half as much as he needs to on an uphill. But, the natural runner also generally speeds up about half as much as he needs to on a downhill. When it comes to hills, surprisingly, it's the natural runner who wants to deviate from his pace as little as possible. That said, remember, the natural runner's pace is a gradually slowing one.

Just to make it simple: Run hills like you're an eighteen-wheeler. But since you don't weigh multiple tons, and you don't have wheels, expect little in the way of momentum when a downhill immediately precedes an uphill. The temptation is to take all the energy recovered from the downhill and immediately expend it on the uphill. Resist the urge. Spread the use of it over the entire remainder of your race.

> **Run hills like you're an 18-wheeler.**

To get the correct slowdown on any uphill, picture the entire remainder of the race at that slope. If you are a mile from the finish, picture the hill a mile long to the finish and race at that pace. This mental picture should get you to slow down to the correct pace for that hill.

Don't panic about how slow it is. It won't seem slow at all when the other runners start dying in front of you. (Some reduce themselves to walking.)

Since it takes a lot of energy to go a little faster, you also save a lot of energy by going a little slower. Stealth racing on a course with hills, you can enjoy a more relaxed race, with a more even flow in the use of your energy.

5
Psychological Race Factors

SIZE OF THE RACE

The size of a race (number of competitors) usually affects the natural runner.

With bigger crowds of runners, there is usually a subconscious elevation of everyone's adrenaline level. It's "in the air." These "butterflies" alone almost always cause the natural runner to start faster than his already too fast start.

The stealth racer, aware of this factor, watches the "lemmings" run away quickly to their collective demise. The natural runner thinks, "This many runners starting this fast can't ALL be wrong." Yes, they can ALL be wrong.

Yes, they can ALL be wrong.

The natural runner who is the most extremely affected by this situation will experience not only the scenario of being passed by other runners, but the ugly scenario of being passed by a LOT of other runners.

Since natural runners are ruled by what they see, finishing the rest of the race like this can be quite a painful ordeal.

Occasionally, there are obvious physical course restrictions to a road race or cross-country race where it could be difficult to pass. The worst situations will occur near the beginning where runners are much more bunched together than later on the course where they are more spread out.

The natural runner will most likely greatly overreact. His coach has probably already noticed this potential bottleneck and emphasized the importance of a fast start. But what the coach probably doesn't realize is that ALL the coaches are going to tell their teams the same thing.

The stealth racer doesn't overreact. If he senses that he will be forced to slow down, he can react similarly to the way he approaches a downhill section on a course. He can throw in a modest surge before being forced into recovery mode. He then can resume his pace for the entire rest of the race catching those who sprinted their start much faster than even they normally would.

Often, even surging before a bottleneck in the course may not be required. If the race is crowded, but not important, the stealth racer can practice passing crowds of slow runners. It is less difficult than most think, and it is an ability that can come in handy.

When "boxed in" it can be easy to move a runner gently out of the way. If you gently rest your hand on his hip (which is at his center of gravity) he will often easily move sideways with little pressure. In case you haven't noticed, a runner when running, is airborne much of the time.

He is an intermittent hover craft. He will often move as easily as a heavy air hockey puck (but only if there is space to move him into, don't cause a giant pile up.)

IMPORTANCE OF THE RACE

The more important a race, the more aggressive the natural runner becomes. This aggressiveness is often fueled by comments from their coach, or from their teammates.

The natural runner will take these pre-race comments and want to IMMEDIATELY, at the start, show that he has gotten the message. He will usually push his too fast start LONGER than he normally would in a less important race.

In this situation, the stealth racer will catch the over-aggressive natural runner later, but pass quicker because their slowdown will be more severe. Unseen to the stealth racer is the fact that he opens up a bigger gap after the pass. The stealth racer should be aware of this, because his teammates can cash in big if tipped off to this phenomena.

Important races are also easier for the stealth racer. He doesn't waste energy fretting about, or trying to guess, what any of his competitors are going to do. Often, the best way to defeat a lot of potential tactics is to ignore them.

But, occasionally, tactics are used successfully against the stealth racer. When they do occur, realize that a reaction of panic in the situation is what can cause a lot of the loss to your performance. Stay relaxed, and just don't make it worse on yourself by getting frustrated. Often, being patient and doing nothing will actually solve a tactical dilemma. Often, patience is NOT your first instinct.

Often, the best way to defeat a lot of potential tactics is to ignore them.

As you get more experienced you will be able to react quicker when situations develop and eventually be able to recognize and avoid circumstances that put you at a disadvantage.

Learn that anything can happen quickly in a race, so pride yourself on your increasing ability to not be surprised. You can analyze more fully what happened to you after your race.

Trying some new strategy or tactic is often not a good idea in big meets. That type of thing should be attempted first in less important races.

Often, when entering large invitational meets where there are no qualifying heats to get to championship finals, entrants are required to submit qualifying times so that they can be grouped with other runners of similar ability. Most runners submit the fastest times that they are allowed. They are under the delusion that they can somehow get "pulled" to a faster time by running against faster runners. Many adhere to this plan regardless of how rarely it helps, and regardless of how often it fails.

The stealth racer just submits his predicted finish time. What this does is usually create the ideal scenario where he is likely to win his heat (always fun) and his even pace will very often produce a last-to-first topnotch performance. This sure beats the natural runner with his often inflated seed time who once again is hoping that THIS TIME he won't slow down.

What is it about pain that is repeatedly self-inflicted that almost everyone forgets? (THIS TIME I will stay up very late and NOT be tired the next day.) (THIS TIME I will consume large quantities of certain substances and NOT regret it the next day.) I guess it's just natural. I guess it's a hard habit to break.

AGE OF RUNNER

The least experienced but mostly the YOUNGEST runners have NO concept of pace.

> *The youngest runners have NO concept of pace.*

This is no big revelation to anyone who has run a road race. When you ran a road race, who were you passing just a little way into, and all throughout, the race? Young runners. And who is that passing you the rest of the way? (Hint: Think a completely different age group.)

Experience is a good teacher. But experience usually gets you only half way there (or only half as fast.)

A quick anecdote:

Two high school freshmen girls about to run their first 400 meter race say, "What do we do, what do we do?" I say, "When the gun goes off, you follow them. When they slow down, you go around them." (They weren't running in lanes.)

When new runners have the "jitters" or the "butter-flies," and may be experiencing adrenaline for the first time, mellow words are required (running is different from most other sports this way.)

I stopped by the starting line two more times. Two more times the same question was frantically asked. Two more times I calmly answered. It's amazing how nerves can scatter the brain.

Anyway, the gun goes off. They did what I said. They passed quite a few of the other girls. It went well. They were happy.

Fast-forward a couple of weeks. I catch their track meet, dreading the prospect that, like other runners, they would now be sprinting to their doom.

Nope. They were doing just fine, still running down competitors, only now with quicker times on the results sheet.

What is it about our FIRST experience with an important race that can shape our way of competing (good or bad) for YEARS? When you think about it, it's only natural. But, once again, running a race is NOT NATURAL. It is a SPORT that you have to LEARN.

TEAM MEMBER OR INDIVIDUAL

Racing as an individual gives you the luxury to experiment in ways that your coach or teammates might not be "comfortable" with. Being a member of a team usually increases the pressure to look good in the eyes of your coach and teammates. This is one area where sports actually does prepare you for the real world.

Many justifications for sports participation are just platitudes. Dealing with a coach is not too different from dealing in the future (or in the present) with a boss. (If you are on an athletic scholarship he IS your boss.)

Most coaches are reasonable, but diplomacy sure helps. You need to figure out what approach works with your coach.

Your coach may not care how you run your race. Enjoy the freedom. If he does have a reaction indicating that he would prefer that you didn't race the way that you did, you have options on how to proceed.

You could get him involved. Have him do the math (divide your time into four equal quarters, or calculate your 100-meter pace.) Have him hold the watch and record your split times. Frequently, this alone will "enlighten" the coach. He may become your biggest fan and collaborator.

I would like to add a serious note to those coaches who have forgiven me for the title of my book: If a coach wants to institute a stealth strategy for his team, I very highly suggest that he let each individual runner decide for themselves (after learning about it in this book, of course.)

The motivation it takes to run a race well (and the motivation it takes to train well) can be quite personal. Like I said before, it only takes a FEW races to tell if stealth racing works for any one particular athlete. It's HARD to break natural running habits, but it's EASY to stop stealth racing.

> *It's HARD to break natural running habits. It's EASY to stop stealth racing.*

If trying to stealth race interferes with a natural runner's ability to give 100% percent, you can return them to their previous ways with a good old-fashioned pep talk and some LOUD encouragement during their race.

I've never liked certain strategies or tactics forced on me when I race, so I wouldn't do the same to anyone else.

Besides, what could be more stealth of a team strategy than to have a combination of stealth racers and natural runners for your opponents to deal with? If they care about YOUR team's strategy, they won't have a clue what you are doing. I think the best team strategy, by default, is to let each runner figure out how to get themselves to the finish line in the least amount of time.

I now return back to runners who want to stealth race and are the main purpose of this book.

If your coach doesn't like the way you pace your race and insists on trusting what he sees (an optical illusion), you may have to "tweak" your pace a bit (start a little too fast) so as not to alarm him. It will probably disrupt your comfort more than it will actually hinder your performance.

If, God forbid, you actually race better by starting a little faster, all the other principles of stealth racing are still at your disposal. As an added bonus, this can actually hide your racing skills from other stealth racers.

But if you wish to stay with your stealth racing in a more pure form (pacing even or negative-splitting,) you may just wear down your coach with your stubbornness (or with the entertainment value to your teammates.)

To a lesser degree, your teammates can become complicit in your strategy.

When stalking your competitor from behind, your teammates can express sympathy for your "slow" performance as they look back at you from the side of the track. They can "cheer" you on in a way that your opponent can hear. "Nice try." "Hang in there." "Don't give up."

Hearing "encouragement" like this can lull your competitor into complacency, unable to see what is happening behind him (like your winking and grinning at the prospect of blowing him off the track.) It might not have much impact on the result, but it can amuse your teammates greatly.

Many top coaches insist that at some distances (mostly races between 400 and 800 meters) the optimum performance comes from running the first half of a race two seconds faster than the second half. This is actually true for a lot of runners.

But the stealth racer approaches this strategy opposite from the way the natural runner does. The natural runner, trying to keep contact with the leaders, HOPES he can avoid slowing through sheer will power. He HOPES he can slow only two seconds.

> *The stealth racer approaches this strategy in the opposite way.*

The stealth racer, however, starts with even or negative splits to break the habit of ONLY following the pack, trusting ONLY what he sees, and being ruled by it. The stealth racer runs his pace INDEPENDENT from the pack. Only after establishing this habit can he THEN attempt slightly more aggressive starts to see if this theory applies to him at these distances.

There is not just ONE best way to race for EVERY runner. Even stealth racing is not the best strategy for every runner. (Remember all the warnings at the beginning of this book?) I just believe that stealth racing is the BEST default strategy to defer to when races begin to go badly.

RELATIVE ABILITY

Your ability compared to the other runners in your race is where the greatest resistance to stealth racing can occur. If you are the best runner, all the attention focuses on you. No one criticizes the winner's strategy. So if you aren't one of the best runners, if you are the OTHER 90%, stealth racing is your golden ticket.

This is where two rules I mentioned before come into play. Runners are ruled by what they SEE. Runners don't RACE, they CHASE.

About the only strategy for the natural runner is to position himself where he expects to finish (I'm faster than this person, but I want to catch that person,) and stay there until he feels like doing something else. In the race, what develops is a phenomena where everyone chases the runner in front of them for as long as they can. This results in individual runners just dropping off the back of the pack due to fatigue.

The fastest runner is not chasing anyone, his pace is not so bad. He has no VISIBLE rabbit taunting him to go any faster. As you go further back in the pack, the temptation gets more pronounced, the effect accumulates. These runners are chasing other runners who themselves are pushing a pace they can't maintain.

When you get back to the slowest runner who may BE 50% slower than the fastest runner, he is usually not STARTING 50% slower, he is usually starting only 20% slower. This, by definition, is way too fast for the slower runners, even though they ALREADY look slow.

As a general rule, the slower runners slow much more than the faster runners do.

> *Slower runners slow much more than faster runners.*

For slower runners, running a bad race is NOT a matter of fitness, it is a matter of not knowing the rhythm of a properly paced race. Even if the slower runner gets in better shape, he is usually stuck in his natural racing rhythm. He will die slowly at a faster pace, but he will still die.

The stealth racer with the less-than-great ability will find that a surprising number of the slowest runners will start FASTER than his race pace. It LOOKS wrong, but he KNOWS he is right. Most of the race, dying rabbits are there to be picked off, with much less pain experienced while doing it.

In a large race with many runners, these first-time stealth racers can feel quite an adrenaline rush passing so many runners so quickly. He may unwittingly speed up and wear himself out too soon. But the next time he tapers his reaction to savor the experience for the entire race.

For the less-talented stealth racer, the "bungee cord" is longer, and frequently makes for a more exhilarating ride. He "falls behind" more runners and "catches" many more from a greater distance back.

The natural runner in these middle-of-a-large-pack races will almost never even APPROACH an evenly paced race (even by accident.) Because of this, the strategy of the less-talented stealth racer almost always somehow looks in these type of races to be even more wrong to most spectators and coaches.

Hey, sometimes no good deed (or strategy) goes unpunished. About all you can do is give them a calculator and the watch and have THEM tell YOU what your split times should be.

Now, one of the biggest failures in competition is completely avoided by stealth racing. There is no place in the race to "zone out." The stealth racer is NOT going to hear the coach yelling at him, "You fell ASLEEP out there!"

It is the natural trap to the natural runner to experience this "zoning out." This occurrence is revealed only when he "wakes up" at the sight of the finish line. He goes from plodding runner to sprinter in two seconds flat. Despite the cheers from the crowd, this is NOT a good thing. Don't blame the runner, he's just doing what comes naturally.

> *It is the natural trap for the natural runner to experience this "zoning out."*

He starts with pre-race jitters, an uncomfortable formation of "butterflies" in his gut. Everyone lines up, and then some guy FIRES A GUN!

By sprinting his discomfort away, he is now flying along in an adrenaline-fueled stampede with a hoard of fellow competitors who are usually wearing spikes. He quickly gets to an acceptable level of fatigue and stays at that level of exertion. He finds an acceptable runner to follow and focuses on their back.

One minute he is near panic. The next minute he is settled into a respectable exertion level, and staring at the back of the runner in front of him. Unchanging feel. Unchanging view. It happens so fast, it's almost a recipe for hypnosis.

The bigger the race, the louder the pep talk from the coach, the higher the adrenaline level goes, and the deeper the "trance" the athlete is thrust into once the race gets going.

No one falls asleep experiencing the "bungee jump" of running a stealth race. The apparent "falling behind" quickly at the start, and more than making up for it during the rest of the race, leaves no place for "sleep." It is up to you whether you "wake" the other runners as you go by.

> *No one falls asleep experiencing the "bungee jump" of running a stealth race.*

In the middle of the race it doesn't make much difference, the natural runners don't have the energy to stay with you very long anyway.

Near the end of the race, it is a different scenario where the other runner may have slowed so much that he has recovered from fatigue. You decide whether passing quickly or passing slowly is the better option. But if he does speed up and beat you to the line, don't beat YOURSELF up. In reality, he is a better runner with greater ability who shouldn't have let you get so close in the first place. Scaring the hell out of him should be reward enough.

6
Racing with Skill

Stealth racing strategy often makes the use of tactics unnecessary, so a definition for tactics is needed that will keep them useful.

Since stealth racing involves the most efficient use of your energy, and by now you are in the habit of ignoring your competitors:

TACTICS involve sacrificing small amounts of your energy to get your competitor to sacrifice large amounts of his.

Any of the many tactics that may be suggested to you can now be analyzed for their usefulness, your amusement, or your enjoyment. Since you are always aware of pace, you can relax and trust your judgment.

PHYSICAL TACTICS

Physical tactics are a matter of where you place your body on the track, and what speed you run once you've placed it there. These tactics come into play when you want to control a race for your benefit. They are more important on indoor tracks than on outdoor tracks.

Now is a good time to address one of the few tactics that the natural runner knows. You run right behind any runner to avoid energy output spent on air resistance. It is called drafting, and it is real. They say it saves you 7% on energy output. Since going a little faster takes a lot of energy, it saves you about 1% on your time (which is significant.)

> *Tactics involve sacrificing small amounts of energy to get your competitor to sacrifice large amounts of his.*

Of course it is significant IF you could draft off of someone for your WHOLE race. It is the LAST tactic that the new stealth racer should engage in because it involves several problems (the MAIN one being not establishing the habit of ignoring your competitors.) Maintaining contact with an even pace can easily be lost in this pursuit. Even the experienced stealth racer can have difficulty finding another runner running at a speed close enough to his pace for very long.

When the natural runner runs his "own" race it usually involves following someone and then trying to speed up at some point. "Running his own race" really means running SOMEONE ELSE'S race until he feels like doing something different.

He doesn't stealth race because he can't SEE even pace. He follows other runners because he CAN see THEM. But he is at the mercy of guessing what those other runners will do, or what pace they will run. If he drafts off the leader, some runner may come up on his outside and block him in, because that runner (and others behind him) have the same strategy. So he runs on the leader's outside shoulder to prevent being blocked, but gives up some of the draft, and runs a longer distance around the turns. All this jostling around and no one is thinking about pace!

> *The natural runner is at the mercy of guessing what the other runners will do.*

Is it too fast?

The stealth racer hangs back unobstructed and maybe drafts off EVERYONE.

Is the pace slow?

The stealth racer has got a pace to keep. He just calmly takes over, and sometimes he will just calmly pull away. Sometimes he won't. Sometimes he becomes the rabbit that they blow off the track with a sprint kick. Sometimes just one or two runners will.

Who cares? The stealth racer probably clocks a decent time, and often gets some respect from his competitors. Either way, these runners who kick past him just prove the point that running a negative split doesn't hurt your performance that much.

Is it medium paced?

This doesn't happen often. The stealth racer just gets as comfortable a position as he can and runs relaxed. He has to decide how relaxed he can remain running in a group of other runners while trying to keep his pace. He can decide if he would rather surge ahead of the pack or drop behind the pack to avoid physical contact. If he senses that the race is "up for grabs," he can just try to make his move before anyone else makes theirs.

The stealth racer can also control a race by running up front. He has no problem with leading the race because he has the intuition telling him what is happening behind him. He's watched it so many times from in back that the racing habits of the other runners have become predictable.

On these less likely occasions when he chooses to lead, it helps immensely for the stealth racer to realize that he is IN THE WAY (especially indoors.) This is a good situation, he MILKS it. He doesn't FLEE from it.

The instinct of the stealth racer becomes the opposite of the natural runner in these tactical situations on the track. When in the lead, the instinct of the natural runner is to FLEE from his pursuers. The tactic of the stealth racer is to back off the pace and DISRUPT his pursuers.

> **When in the lead, the instinct of the stealth racer is the opposite of the natural runner.**

Get them to run wide on turns. Get them to accelerate and decelerate. Get them to panic. Sometimes even when you know you can beat them anyway, slow them down for your teammates to pick off.

The stealth racer is not overly worried about being passed by his pursuers, because he knows where on the track this is most likely to occur. And where it is less likely, he will have the advantage.

The stealth racer knows that his pursuers are NOT likely to try to pass on a turn (where they have to run faster while running extra distance.) He knows that they WILL try to pass on a straightaway.

So the stealth racer slows going into and through the turns, and he accelerates coming off the turns and through the straightaways. His gentle surging and slowing disrupts his pursuers from any easy passing attempts. Passing HIM is going to have a steep cost.

EXTRA acceleration is needed for a pursuer to complete a pass, and EXTRA slowing (even braking) may be needed if running a wide turn is to be avoided by the pursuer. The stealth racer can hold off his challengers because he has the ENERGY to do it. Energy to accelerate is the hidden benefit (hidden to natural runners) of slowing the pace of a race. When it's time to go, the stealth racer can accelerate to a pace he can maintain to the finish, while most of his pursuers will be too worn out to keep up.

There is more than one way to run a stealth race. The stealth racer has options. Most natural runners don't realize that there are any options. And many of them don't know how to make adjustments when the circumstances of the race change.

Things often happen quickly in a race, stealth racers can adjust for the unexpected. If the stealth racer can't adjust quickly enough, it's not a big deal, he has more races in his future, and now, more experience to handle situations as they arise.

PSYCHOLOGICAL TACTICS

Psychological tactics involve using the natural instincts of the natural runner against him. This involves the stealth racer focusing on what the natural runner will SEE, because the natural runner is ruled by it. These tactics are more important in longer races.

These tactics deal with the fact that fatigue and pain are REALITIES that must be dealt with. This seems to be a reality that natural runners want to pretend doesn't exist. They want to pretend that fatigue can be overcome with will power alone and that there is nothing physical about it.

The stealth racer avoids this folly knowing it makes about as much sense as repeatedly stomping on the gas pedal when a car has run out of gas. Only the smallest amounts of fatigue can be "wished away" in this manner.

When running against a natural runner in longer races, tactics depend on what level of a fatigue "coma" he has put himself into.

If it is an EARLY stage of a race you can goad him into speeding up when he still feels he has energy to burn (he doesn't.)

Why make his race worse? You may have teammates behind you who can catch him only if he has a bad race. Passing him slowly may entice him to go with you. Be friendly in your prodding, you want all your psychological tactics to be stealth. He will have no clue how much your "help" has hurt him.

> **The natural runner will have no clue how much your "help" has hurt him.**

In the middle stages of the race, the comatose natural runner is more likely to be resigned to his condition. However you pass him at this point is not likely to affect him at all.

It is frequently at this point that his coach will yell at him. If he speeds up as a result, all the better for your amusement, he will soon slow WAY down. He already blew his race with a fast start. Even the coach can't fix that, fatigue is REAL.

It also can be quite amusing to listen to WHAT the natural runner's coach is yelling. The frustration level of an unexperienced coach will be heard proportionally to the volume of his voice.

He WANTS to help his athletes, he often just doesn't know HOW. Usually the only benefit to the athlete is that he is woken up for a short time before resuming comatose running.

Also, friendly encouraging of the natural runner can be used at any point on the course where there is a decent sized hill. If you verbally reveal your slower pace running up hills as a weakness, you may spur him into overconfidence that he will break away from you at this point. It is important to express your admiration for his effort as you pass him a short while later.

In the later stages of the race, the comatose natural runner may awaken and realize he has some energy left (a slow enough pace will produce physical recovery.) You can pass him slowly (let him keep sleeping,) pass him fast (don't let him even think about trying to keep up,) or maybe just swing wide (he might not even notice you.)

If it is your teammate, you may want to wake him. (Or maybe not. Maybe he doesn't LIKE the way you race.)

Once again, ignore those runners who sprint by you at the sight of the finish line. They are runners with more ability than you who just don't know how to race.

7
Strategy

The stealth strategy is to go from the start line to the finish line with the most efficient use of all your energy. This should produce your best time. This is the basis from which all stealth racing begins. Other runners are just obstacles in your pursuit that are usually easy to negotiate.

> *The stealth strategy is to go from the start to the finish with the most efficient use of all your energy.*

Knowing how to run a race to your best possible time is a great (and usually rare) ability. Recognizing which of your tendencies you are more "naturally" susceptible to is also important. You can adjust your approach as you see these factors come into play.

As you become a better runner, you also become better at going ALL OUT. Sometimes you don't WANT to go all out. Sometimes you SHOULDN'T go all out. Sometimes you have another race to run. Sometimes you have a more important race coming up.

Sometimes the strategy involves getting a "good enough" result with the least amount of exertion (like racing qualifying heats to advance to the final.)

You have a number of options to choose from. You can run race pace (for your best expected performance) until you are clear of who you need to beat, and then slow down as you look over your shoulder. Or, if you like to keep the competition in front of you where you can see them, you can plot a negative-split stealth race where you run each split a little faster.

You often have a difficult decision to make. Do I go all out to make it to the final? Or do I run what I will, so that if I make it to the final, I can still run a respectable race?

My preference (since natural runners usually go with the first option) is to go for the second (I'm stubborn that way.) Your patience can be your strength, you can wait for another day if it doesn't work out.

Or maybe you can't wait. Maybe your whole goal IS to make it to the final.

If you do find yourself in the lead (or a qualifying position) in the final stretch of a qualifying heat, it makes sense to veer on a diagonal toward the outside lanes so that it is easier for you to spot someone moving up from behind. Usually the natural runner doesn't do the math.

Moving out seven lanes (seven meters) on a 100-meter straightaway doesn't add seven meters to your distance to the finish line, it adds only ten inches. I think it's the Pythagorean Theorem that would say, "It's worth it, use it." I told you stealth racing was math.

Tactics and strategies often suggested by other coaches and runners involve a phrase that starts with something like, "Well, if you want to win the race, you need to..."

Ignore them. Who wins the race is rarely determined by who wants it the most (we just wish it was that way.) Since desire can't be measured, most assume it to be so. They like the sound of the platitudes it creates.

> *Who wins the race is rarely determined by who wants it the most.*

Those who watch races are so focused on what is going on up front that they usually only know the tactics that work for the few runners in any race that have a chance of winning. That's why most coaches are so occupied with the tactic of maintaining contact with the leaders. It can only work for the few runners who most observers are so focused on.

For those who stealth race, the stealth strategy works regardless of ability.

Most automatically assume that those who win races race well. Race results are more a factor of ability and training than on racing skills. That is why this topic is so often overlooked or unexamined (until now, that is.)

Often a runner can easily win WITHOUT good racing skills if his performance is due to his natural ability and training. Sometimes it is NOT best to emulate the strategy or tactics of a great runner. It could just be that he is just plain FAST.

> *The stealth strategy works regardless of ability.*

In many great breakout race performances, the result is a surprise to the athlete. Not all great races are a result of goal-setting and focusing on one particular meet. Stealth racers accept the satisfaction of consistently getting their optimum performance on any day and enjoying the results it produces.

Besides, winning the race is NOT the goal in every race. For instance, if you are the fifth man on a good cross-country team, you can't be risking the team result by "taking your shot" at the almost total impossibility of winning. As the fifth man, you usually are the MOST important man concerning team score.

In a big meet, if your top runner has a bad race, it only costs your team a few points (score is determined by place, not time.) If the fifth runner has a bad race, it will probably cost his team at least twice as much (there are a lot more places to lose because there are a lot more other runners back there in the pack to take them.) Stealth racing is the BEST way to prevent a poor performance that could jeopardize your team.

> **Stealth racing is the BEST way to prevent a poor performance that could jeopardize your team.**

The major point that usually ONLY the stealth racer knows is that options open up the more energy you have. You have more energy if you start SLOWER not FASTER.

Your only option if you're tired is trying to maintain your pace. Or slow down. In reality, those are not options. It's the drudgery that the natural runner finishes most of his races with.

Whereas the stealth racer knows how to capitalize on leading a race, he is probably the only one who knows all the benefits of running in back. Sometimes the stealth racer finds himself running behind only one runner who may or may not be pacing too badly. The natural runner will almost always run next to, on the shoulder of, or directly behind this leader.

> *The stealth racer is probably the only one who knows all the benefits of running in back.*

The stealth racer knows another option. Instead of drafting, he can stay back away from the leader (even maybe out of earshot), so that the leader is unaware of his movements, or even of his presence (out of sight, out of mind.) He may even be drifting slowly into a fatigue "coma" that only your presence may keep him out of.

The stealth racer can then stalk his prey from this not too close, not too far distance, pondering when and how to attack. Also, this gap between him and the leader gives the stealth racer room for acceleration, and a surprise to the leader that can be extremely difficult to react to.

When, leading early in a race, the stealth racer may be surprised at how good it feels to be in the spotlight, and feeling his form take on a new level of efficiency and style. But he is not addicted to it like the natural runner. He can take that same form to the back of the pack.

In back, the stealth racer has "the best seat in the house" to watch the race that he is IN. He is rarely caught off guard because he isn't like the natural runner who is up front usually running "blind."

From in back, his close range observation of the competition begins to give him an almost "sixth sense" of what they CAN do, or sometimes even what they WILL do. HE can see THEM, THEY can't see HIM. The stealth runner won't let this view of his competitors CONTROL him, but he will let it ALERT him of possibilities.

From time to time, the stealth racer knows ahead of time how his race is going to finish. This level of knowing the outcome before it happens (especially if the result ends up in him winning) is one of the great "being in the zone" experiences that the stealth runner will never forget.

8
Mental Training

Just like the stealth racer's strategy often (but not always) makes the use of tactics unnecessary, the stealth racer's strategy often makes most standard mental approaches unnecessary. Even a stealth racer needs some extra help when some races cause extra anxiety.

Now often, the mental aspect of racing is treated with no more than some platitude about "mental toughness." The usual line of thinking does not really focus on a mental exercise but an emotional one. Most talk is usually geared toward "psyching up" an athlete to give his maximum effort when experiencing maximum distress. These types of pep talks work better in the training realm of the sport, and even then they need to be set in the context of consistency and patience while avoiding overtraining.

In a race, however, the mental toughness required to push through the pain of fatigue is largely taken care of by the stealth strategy. Some natural runners fall into the trap of thinking that pain is the goal and that more pain equals faster times. The stealth racer knows that this is NOT the case. The stealth racer treats the pain of fatigue as information for pacing during the race, not an enemy to be defeated.

> *Mental toughness is largely taken care of by the stealth strategy.*

The natural runner often brings instincts, habits, and teachings with him from other sports. Many of these need to be modified or eliminated for the sport of running.

A race is different from a game. The most important difference identified early in this book is aggressiveness. In a lot of sports aggressiveness is required all throughout the contest. And yet over-aggressiveness is often penalized.

Aggressiveness is more of an emotional function that is ratcheted up just BEFORE the game. This is often done with rituals that can't usually be performed DURING the game. If you are an aggressive person and the reason WHY you race is for the outlet of that aggression you need to moderate it to be a stealth racer.

In most team sports, unlike in running, if your anxiety level is very high, you calm down as soon as the game begins. Your first hit, your first contact with anything, settles you down and you're ready to play. You are constantly stopping and starting and getting into the rhythm of the game.

It is not so in running. When the race starts it does not stop. When the race stops it does not start again. It's over. No breaks. No time-outs. No wonder runners get nervous to the point of queasiness.

So what do you do?

Like the effort level in your race, your level of aggression should be almost zero at the start and as high as you want at the end. If you are not an aggressive person you have an advantage. In most races, just by focusing on your level of effort, you are lured into becoming aggressive as you find yourself looking ahead for more and more runners to catch before reaching the finish line. The stealth racer is confident, he is not nearly as worried as the natural runner is about having a poor effort.

Usually for all athletes (especially the least experienced), most of the difficulties occur before the race. Nervous anticipation is required before competing at your highest level or else your performance is just reduced to a time trial. A time trial is just information on your level of fitness.

A race result goes on the permanent record! You don't know where they keep it, but it will be kept somewhere for anyone to look up for decades to come. You just know subconsciously that a race IS important.

In this context anxiety is a GOOD thing, you want to be ANXIOUS for the competition to start. For the natural runner, anxiety is often a BAD thing, he is anxious about avoiding a BAD race.

Anxiety is a GOOD thing, you WANT to be anxious for the competition to start.

What you need to know is how to moderate your anxiety level. Every athlete is different in this regard. Some like a ritual that tunes out the surrounding stimulus of the event. Some take in the atmosphere and adjust. If your team has pre-race rituals, you can regulate your level of participation (jump right in with excitement or just go through the motions, the difference isn't always noticeable to others.)

For the stealth racer the mental preparation is aimed at producing control and relaxation during the race. The whole mental approach is merely a matter of collecting words or phrases and mental pictures that produce this result for you. The best way I have found to accomplish this is by thinking of the mind and the body as two separate entities. Replace thoughts like "I am really nervous" with "my stomach feels queasy, it always does that, but I'm fine."

Soon, you expect the nervousness, you anticipate that anxious feeling. It is like your body is telling you, "Adrenaline levels are at full capacity for a high performance level and awaiting ignition. Relax, we are now switching to standby mode."

Natural runners are more likely to use "natural" mental pictures (graceful animals or other runners.) The stealth racer is more likely to use mental pictures of machines that can easily be controlled. Since you are not a machine, this approach helps the stealth racer control his natural impulses instead of being overcome by them.

Get creative with your concepts for use during your race. For example, picture your body as a running machine that fits like a light, flexible suit with all controls centered in your brain. You think it, your body does it. If you just think about speeding up, your body will feel the impulse to speed up.

If it is able, your body will respond to your thoughts, especially detailed vivid thoughts. In fact, if you take a second to think first, instead of act first, your body will respond better.

You can create any feature you want for your "running machine." You can think of your legs as "wheels" that just roll beneath you. If you picture your "running machine" having a cruise control, you can picture yourself clicking it on, leaning back, and enjoying the ride inside. If you want a quick acceleration, you can picture having a brick handy to drop onto your accelerator. Have fun seeing how your body responds to whatever crazy thing you can concoct in your imagination (just to be clear, we're talking about SPORTS here, not any other kind of recreation.)

In running, mental images quickly produce a level of relaxation with one simple vision that regulating numerous separate physical movements usually cannot.

> **Mental images produce a level of relaxation that regulating numerous separate physical movements cannot.**

However, if you don't think anything, your body will, out of habit, just do what it always does.

Your body gives you information. It tells you how much energy you have left to use. It might tell you how much adrenaline is in reserve. It can be a very thrilling surprise if you happen to underestimate either of these capacities.

This kind of mental imaging can be practiced at any time you are running. Higher levels of concentration, relaxation, efficiency, comfort, and performance may just be as close as a few of the right thoughts, imaginatively created in your own mind.

9
The Finish Line

Relax. Stealth racing is simple.

Initially it's just the three words:

Pace yourself. Evenly.

Once you get that down you could have figured out the rest on your own. I just thought I'd save you years of figuring time. You may not have the ability of a top athlete, but you can now develop the racing skills of one a lot quicker.

This book doubles as a reference. You don't have to memorize it, and you barely have to study it. You can refer back to it when almost anything comes up. It also gives you logic and reason for your defense if you are in need of it.

Take your time learning to be a stealth racer, no one's watching (unless, of course, you TOLD them.)

Don't worry about making mistakes. Learning what you did, and figuring out how to correct it, will break up the monotony of being successful ALL the time.

Eventually you will make your own discoveries not even mentioned in this book.

Once you are established as a consistent stealth racer, you can employ any strategy or tactic you wish. Being always AWARE of your pace, you can adjust, abandon, or switch tactics and strategies mid-race with little delay. You are not locked into pre-race decisions made by you or your coach.

> *You are not locked into pre-race decisions made by you or your coach.*

Though I am no expert on workouts or training philosophies, I do have an opinion on the level of commitment and devotion to the sport and the work it takes to be at your best.

I say you should pace your career like you pace your races. Long careers require patience and consistency and having something in reserve for "turning it up a notch" if you need to.

Just like in a race, you can't go all out all the time.

> *Pace your career like you pace your races.*

And just like the correct race pace that feels easy becomes taxing when you are consistent mile after mile, a moderate training regimen becomes strenuous enough when you are faithful to it month after month.

Fatigue and injuries always await the impatient runner.

Finding enjoyment in your training helps your motivation to continue running. It is my hope that stealth racing will help your enjoyment of competition far beyond the actual improvement of your performance. I believe most of that will come more as a long term byproduct as you avoid the pitfalls of discouragement and burnout that often plagues the aggressive natural runner.

I now await my critics, and encourage them to write many books. After all, nothing would take the fun out of stealth racing more than if EVERYBODY did it.

Comments? Questions? E-mail me.

Rick Smith

Stealthracer57@hotmail.com.